Together We Pray

Together We Pray

*A Prayer Book
for Families*

J. BRADLEY WIGGER

CHALICE
PRESS
ST. LOUIS, MISSOURI

Cover image: Getty Images
Cover and interior design: Elizabeth Wright

Visit Chalice Press on the World Wide Web at
www.chalicepress.com

10 9 8 7 6 5 4 3 2 1   05   06   07   08   09

Library of Congress Cataloging–in–Publication Data

Wigger, J. Bradley.
  Together we pray : a prayer book for families / J. Bradley Wigger.
      p. cm.
  Includes index.
  ISBN 13: 978-0-827236-46-8 (pbk. : alk. paper)
  ISBN 10: 0-827236-46-8
  1. Family—Prayer-books and devotions—English. 2. Family—Religious
life. 3. Prayers. I. Title.
  BV255.W475 2005
  249—dc22

                                                                2004025390
                    Printed in the United States of America

To Mom and Dad, Jim and Emily Wigger,
who first taught me to pray and read.

Contents

Acknowledgments

I am deeply grateful to friends and family who encouraged this project along its way. I particularly thank Laura March, Sarah Tasic, Trent Butler, and the late Jane McAvoy for their logistical and editorial support. Jane is terribly missed.

The roots of this project go back a decade when my wife, Jane Larsen-Wigger, and I were looking for resources to support our own prayer lives at home with our children, Cora and David. We began to imagine writing something together, which hasn't happened yet, but on this book Jane provided vital help and feedback all the same. Jane, David, and Cora were wonderful about hearing and actually praying many of these prayers with me. Thank you so much.

A Word about the Translation

All the quotes from the psalms are translations from the original Hebrew language and taken from the *New Revised Standard Version Bible*.

This translation uses the word Lord (in small caps) where the holy name of God appears in the texts. This is the name revealed to Moses in the book of Exodus, sometimes translated, "I Am" or "I Am Who I Am" (see Exodus 3). Traditionally the name itself is not spoken, and the word *adonai* (Hebrew for "lord") is used instead, out of respect for the holiness of the One who is beyond any name. Add to this the rich variety of images, names, and descriptions the psalms offer, our sense of who this is deepens even as it is humbled.

General Introduction

Prayer Rhythms

Breathe in. Breathe out. Breathing is the beginning of prayer.

Beneath every word, beneath every prayer, the breath of life moves in and out and through us. In the Hebrew language of the book of Psalms, the word for breath, *ruach*, also means spirit. Prayers are spirited words moving in and out and through us. Prayer is breathing deeply in the Spirit of Life.

While there are many kinds of prayer and many ways of praying, the prayers offered in this book are rooted in the psalms of the Bible, scripture shared by Jews and Christians alike. The prayers are not the psalms themselves. Rather, these prayers are inspired by the psalms, much as hymns, devotions, and sermons have been for some 3,000 years.

Like breathing, the psalms reveal a basic rhythm in prayer, two crucial movements reflected in this book. Inhaling, we breathe in the blessings of life flowing from God, strengthening us with beauty, joy, healing, and comfort, for example. Exhaling, we breathe out good things as well, such as care, compassion, and concern for a larger world that desperately needs loving attention.

1

In general then, the prayers of this book reflect a rhythm found in the psalms. The table prayers tend to inhale while the devotional prayers tend to exhale. Infused throughout this rhythm are praise and thanksgiving. In fact, the book of Psalms culminates with everything that breathes praising God—hallelujah!

Perhaps this reveals why we breathe at all.

The Prayers and Their Uses

Memory Prayers

The prayers of this book are for people of all ages. They are sensitive to households where children and their often-harried parents eat and live. For families who continuously feel on the edge of chaos, stopping for a moment to breathe—pausing and expressing thanks and gratitude to God—can be very powerful even if relatively brief. The memory prayers (for the table and for bedtime, the first and last sections) may be particularly helpful. They are written to be used with those who do not read, young children for example, but also older children or adults with linguistic or developmental challenges, so that they, too, can have a collection of prayers available. These prayers, while sometimes a bit playful, nonetheless echo the joys and concerns of particular psalms.

General Introduction

Table and Devotional Prayers

While the *Table Prayers for Mealtime* are written as blessings for a meal, the *Devotional Prayers of Joy and Care* have greater flexibility. They can certainly be used at the table just as the other table prayers. They would be very appropriate to use at the end of a meal, marking the beginning and end of this sacred time at table. But they could be used as part of a special devotional time, perhaps at the beginning or end of the day.

The table prayers tend to celebrate the good things of life just as the psalms do—food, joy, home, love, and more. The devotional prayers pick up from the psalms an intense concern for the people and places where suffering and injustice run rampant, not just where we live, but around the world. Tough stuff, but crucial to the holy rhythms of a living faith.

In each of these larger sections, a line or two from the particular psalm inspiring the prayer is provided. If you were to read the entire psalm, you would find more allusions and reflections of the psalm at work in the prayer. On the other end, all the prayers, including the memory prayers, are left open, without an "Amen" or other conclusion. This is to make room for special concerns, joys, or prayer traditions you may want to incorporate.

You may find other ways or times to use these prayers or the psalms themselves. I hope so. I believe scripture and prayer deepen life. When our hearts focus upon the holy, even for a moment, the world opens up in powerful ways. Our lives are touched with gratitude and compassion alike. In other words, prayer expresses and cultivates love.

May God bless your tables and this world with grace.

Section I

Table Prayers for Mealtime

Introduction to Table Prayers

While the psalms stretch our imaginations to the heavens and beyond, they continue to take us right back to earth. Concrete concerns such as shelter and food, safety and health, are always at hand. Abstract terms like wonder, injustice, or joy are made real and vivid through images of grape vineyards and dripping honey, waste pits and animal snares, singing worshipers and smiling faces. Abstract and concrete images alike are used to name and describe God, the One who is ultimately beyond, or more than, any human term. Yet this God is as near as the food we eat or the love we share.

Whether bowing our heads or lifting them, to pray is to glimpse the heights and depths of the wonder at work in the universe. Whether holding, folding, or lifting our hands to the sky, to pray is to embrace the grace touching our lives. Whether our words are concrete or abstract, shouted, whispered, or even silent, to pray is to breathe praise to the Spirit who breathes life into us and into all creation.

Mealtimes are special. They invite children and adults alike to appreciate the immediate, real gifts of life at hand; mealtimes invite us all to stretch our gratitude to the heavens and beyond.

Enjoy.

Table Memory Prayers

Trees and Rivers

(Inspired by Psalm 1)

For fruit from the trees
and plants by the river,
we thank you God,
forever and ever.

It's All Good

(Inspired by Psalm 16)

Bless this table,
bless this food.
Bless you God,
for it's all good.

Taste and See

(Inspired by Psalm 34)

God makes us happy
     for home and for food.
O taste and see
     that the LORD is good.

Bless the Land

(Inspired by Psalm 36)

Bless the land,
     and bless the bread.
May the whole wide world
     today be fed.

Praise God Again

(Inspired by Psalm 65)

Let it shine
    and let it rain.
Let the earth
    praise God again.

Help the Poor

(Inspired by Psalm 70)

Great is the One
    who helps the poor.
Great is our God
    who loves evermore.

Heavenly Bread

(Inspired by Psalm 78)

God spreads a table
  so we will be fed
  with the water of life
  and heavenly bread.

Table Prayers

Goodness

They are like trees
*   planted by streams of water,*
which yield their fruit in its season,
*   and their leaves do not wither. (Psalm 1:3)*

O God of goodness,
    bless this table
    and those planted around,
    like an orchard growing
    in the garden of life.

As our bodies delight
    in the fruits of your earth,
    may our lives flow with goodness
    like a mighty river.

Shining Face

"Let the light of your face shine on us, O Lord!"
You have put gladness in my heart
* more than when their grain and wine abound.*
* (Psalm 4:6b, 7)*

God of gladness,
let the light of your face shine on us

>   when we lie down and when we rise,
>   when we work and when we rest,
>   when we eat and when we smile,
>   when we cry and when we dream.

Let the light of your face shine on us, we pray.
Let the light of your grace shine on the world.

Crowned with Glory

O LORD, our Sovereign,
how majestic is your name in all the earth!
(Psalm 8:1a)

Great God of creation,
we are stunned by the heavens
and amazed by the earth—
the moon and the stars glow with majesty;
rivers and seas sparkle with glory;
fields and forests abound with honor.

We give you thanks, God of grandeur,
for by your hand, babies and children are majestic;
by your decree, old people and young are glorious;
by your grace, our thoughts and our bodies abound
with honor.

Holy Sovereign, how majestic is your name.
Crown this meal and honor our life together
with the glory of your creation.

Dwelling

O Lord, who may abide in your tent?
Who may dwell on your holy hill? (Psalm 15:1)

O God of dwelling,
    bless this meal and our home
        by your holy presence.

Help us to abide with you and to do what is right:
    to spread the truth,
    to stand by our promises,
    to honor one another,
    to defend the innocent,
    to lend help,
    to respect you.

As our bodies live by the good things of this table,
    may our souls live by
    truth, honor, care, and respect.

May we dwell with you forever.

Holding Hands

Therefore my heart is glad, and my soul rejoices;
my body also rests secure. (Psalm 16:9)

[holding hands]

To the One who secures our lives, we pray.

Hold us in your hand,
    as we hold hands with one another.

Move our hearts to love;
    stir our souls to celebrate;
    and bless our bodies with rest.

For the hand that guides us
    on the way of life,
and for the fullness of joy
    we know in your presence,
we are forever grateful.

Gold

The heavens are telling the glory of God.
(Psalm 19:1a)

As the sun blazes a path
        through the sky,
        set our hearts on fire
        for your way, Holy One.

As the stars soften the world at night,
        let our words
        whisper the wisdom of God.

More precious than gold,
        sweeter than dripping honey,
        is the law of the righteous One.

May this meal
        and our time together
        set us right, Holy God.

The Rock

Let the words of my mouth and the meditation
of my heart
be acceptable to you,
O LORD, my rock and my redeemer.
(Psalm 19:14)

Let the words of our mouths
and the meditations of our hearts;
let the food of this table
and our days together;
let our laughter and tears,
our play and our studies,
our hopes and our dreams,
our loves and our lives
be acceptable to you, Holy God,
our rock and redeemer.

The Shepherd

*The LORD is my shepherd, I shall not want.
  (Psalm 23:1)*

O God, our loving comfort,
    anoint this table with goodness;
    prepare our homes with mercy;
    and restore our souls with life.

May we dwell with you forever.

The Voice

The voice of the LORD flashes forth flames of fire.
(Psalm 29:7)

Glory to you, mighty God,
    ruler of heaven and earth.

To your thundering word,
    giant trees bend and cattle go wild.
To your flaming voice,
    great nations yield
    and small ones live in peace.

Bless us today, majestic God,
    with the good things of the earth.
Loosen us, we pray,
    to bend to your word
    and to go wild for peace.

Acceptance

Happy are those whose transgression is forgiven,
whose sin is covered. (Psalm 32:1)

We praise you today, gracious God,
   we praise you today.

Your love is so steady, and our joy is so great.
You accept our confession and forgive us so freely.
You strengthen our bodies and awaken our minds.
You deliver us from distress and teach us to trust
      your ways.

We praise you today, gracious God,
   we praise you today.

O Taste and See

*O taste and see that the L*ORD *is good.*
(Psalm 34:8a)

We will bless you, Holy Redeemer, at all times;
    we will praise you and magnify your holy name.

You hear our cries
    and take our fears away.
You see our faces
    and take our shame away.
You heal us to the bone
    and protect our broken spirits.

We will bless you, Holy Refuge, at all times;
    we will praise you and magnify your holy name.

You make life taste good,
    with truth, with peace, with desire.
You make our faces beam
    and fill our days with joy.
Bless you, Holy God.

Milk and Honey

Do not fret—it leads only to evil. (Psalm 37:8b)

God of the poor,
    hold us upright and relieve us from fretting.

Walk us, we pray, to the land where you dwell:
    the land where milk and honey flow with
        abandon,
    the land where your people give generously to
        all who have need,
    the land where wicked ways and oppression
        vanish like smoke.

God of the children,
bless the bread we eat from this good earth;
bless every child by the land,
so no child must beg and no child must fret.

Bless this world and make it peaceable.

Hope

As a deer longs for flowing streams,
* so my soul longs for you, O God. (Psalm 42:1)*

O God, our rock, we hope in you.

When our mouths are parched and our bodies
        ache, we hope.
When our hearts are troubled and our minds
        noisy, we hope.
When our souls long for living water, we hope in
        you, O God.

Come, mighty one,
    flood our souls with gladness,
    and shower creation with steadfast love.
Come, mighty one,
    thunder the earth with your song,
    and let the oceans swell with thanksgiving.

O God, our rock, we hope in you.

Home

Clap your hands, all you peoples;
shout to God with loud songs of joy. (Psalm 47:1)

Take your throne, majestic God,
    and let the world praise you.

Let the nations clap;
    let the people sing;
    let every voice shout for joy.

Take your throne, Most High,
    take your chair and sit.
Sit with us, we pray,
    dwell with your people—right here, right now.

Be at home.

Heart

My heart is steadfast, O God,
my heart is steadfast. (Psalm 57:7a)

Merciful God,
    our hearts are pounding with praise and gratitude.

As your love reaches to the mountains,
    our hearts pound.
As your love reaches to the clouds,
    our hearts pound.
As your love reaches to the moon, the sun, the planets,
        the stars—
    beyond all we know—our hearts praise you.

God Most High,
    reach to us, we pray.

Touch our souls with joy
    and this table with love.
Awaken our hearts to grateful living,
    and they will beat praise, upon praise, upon praise,
        upon praise.

A Rich Feast

My soul is satisfied as with a rich feast,
and my mouth praises you with joyful lips.
(Psalm 63:5)

O God our help, bless you.

When we are thirsty,
    you pour water.
When we are hungry,
    you offer good food to eat.
When we are tired,
    you hold us up.
When we are hurting,
    you care.

Feast with us today, God of love,
    so our lips can celebrate your glory.

Bless you.

A Spacious Place

Make a joyful noise to God, all the earth…
you have brought us out to a spacious place.
   (Psalm 66:1,12b)

O God of steadfast love,
      let the earth praise you;
      let all the earth sing glory to you.

As we devote our home to hospitality,
      accept our table as a joyful noise.
As we offer our lips in praise,
      accept our hearts as a spacious place for mercy.

O God of steadfast love,
      bless you.
Let all the earth bless you.

Generations

Upon you I have leaned from my birth;
it was you who took me from my mother's womb.
(Psalm 71:6a)

God, our rock and refuge,
    at this table gather young and old
    with mouths full of praise
    and hearts beaming with glory.

For babies rest in you for hope,
    and children learn to trust.
For the gray know comfort,
    and the old are never forsaken.

From one day to the next,
    from one generation to another,
we celebrate the wonder of God,
    our rock and refuge.

Grain

May there be abundance of grain in the land;
may it wave on the tops of the mountains;
may its fruit be like Lebanon;
and may people blossom in the cities
like the grass of the field. (Psalm 72:16)

O God of abundant life,
may your glory fill every land
and your justice rule the nations;
may prosperity rain down from the heavens,
and peace blossom in every field on the earth.

Deliver those who cry, we pray.
Break oppression and violence with love.
Feed every poor child under the sun,
help all in need,
and let blessing flow from sea to sea.

Blessed be the God of abundance,
whose grain feeds the world.

Manna

"Can God spread a table in the wilderness?"
(Psalm 78:19b)

O God of Israel,
    we recall today your wonders and give you thanks.

May the bread we eat help us remember
    how you fed our ancestors in the wilderness,
    how you rained manna down—
        that grain of heaven,
        that bread of angels.

May the water we drink help us remember
    how you gave life to our ancestors in the desert,
  splitting rocks with deep springs,
    making water flow like a river.

For the grain of heaven and the rivers of life,
    we give you thanks.

Honey from the Rock

*"I would feed you with the finest of the wheat,
and with honey from the rock I would satisfy you."
(Psalm 81:16)*

O God, our strength,
    open our ears, and fill them with your voice;
    open our hearts, and fill them with joy;
    open our mouths, and fill them with praise.

For you lift our burdens, and you satisfy our souls
    with the finest wheat,
    with honey from the rock.

Let trumpets blow; let harps sing sweetly.
Let thanksgiving sweep across the land.

Nesting

Happy are those who live in your house,
ever singing your praise. (Psalm 84:4)

Holy God, our sun and shield,
how beautiful is your home
    the temple where you dwell,
    the city where you rule,
    the valley filled with springs,
    the earth bursting with joy.

As the swallow nests,
    your presence shelters the vulnerable.
As the sparrow tends her young,
    your presence strengthens the body
    and makes every heart happy.

Bless this home and these bodies;
bless this table and this world
    with your nesting presence.

Make them beautiful, we pray.

Revival

Steadfast love and faithfulness will meet;
  righteousness and peace will kiss each other.
  (Psalm 85:10)

O God of salvation,
    restore us today and forgive our sins;
    revive our bodies with the good harvest
        from your earth;
    renew us, we pray, with the bread of peace.

May your steadfast love kiss this home
    and touch this table.
May your glory dwell in the lands
    and flood the skies.
And may the springs of love
    refresh our life together.

Heaven and Earth

The heavens are yours, the earth also is yours;
the world and all that is in it—
  you have founded them. (Psalm 89:11)

O God of David,
    let every generation remember
    and every mouth proclaim forever
    your steadfast love that founds heaven
        and earth.

Let the heavens praise you
    with glowing moons and shooting stars.
Let the oceans praise you
    with raging waves and peaceful waters.

Let north and south praise you.
Let the beginning and the end praise you.
Let righteousness and justice praise you.
Let our lives and our lips praise you.

Let every generation remember
    and every mouth proclaim forever
    your steadfast love that founds heaven
        and earth.

Bearing Fruit

The righteous flourish like the palm tree,
    and grow like a cedar in Lebanon. (Psalm 92:12)

Your works are great, faithful God,
    and your thoughts overwhelm us.

By your hand good things happen:
    righteousness grows like a thousand-ringed tree,
    and grace blooms like the garden of Eden.

Let the good things of this table—
    the food, the company, the joy—
help us to bear the fruits of love
    in your world.

Soft Hearts

O come, let us worship and bow down…
  Do not harden your hearts. (Psalm 95:6a, 8a)

Soften our hearts, mighty God,
  that we may hear your voice
  and see the works of your hand.
Soften our hearts, great maker,
  that we may rest in you,
  giving thanks.

As we bow to you in praise today,
  we are grateful for the hand
  that sculpts mountains and shapes seas.
As we bow to you in praise, great shepherd,
  lead us to the land of rest,
where our bodies feed on thanksgiving
  and our hearts are at ease in your presence.

Dust

The LORD is merciful and gracious,
   slow to anger and abounding in steadfast love.
(Psalm 103:8)

God of all mercy,
 Let this food and our days
    remind us of your benefits.
Renew our table and this time together
    with love and grace.

At every moment you remember we are dust,
    blowing through the desert, flitting about the stars.
You remember we are dust,
    dried up by hatred and burned out by injustice.

Bless you, O God of compassion,
    for creating life from the dust—
    for healing, forgiving, redeeming
       us back to life.
In every moment, your mercy blows us home to love.
We give you thanks.

Springs

You cause the grass to grow for the cattle,
and plants for people to use,
to bring forth food from the earth.
(Psalm 104:14)

Bless the Holy One,
in whom there is life.

As fresh springs well up from the earth,
cool rivers flow down from the mountains.
With every drink of water, we bless the Holy One,
in whom there is life.

As plants and grasses grow to feed a hungry planet,
bread and wine make the heart glad to be alive.
With every meal, we bless the Holy One,
in whom there is life.

The Promised Land

[God] opened the rock, and water gushed out;
   it flowed through the desert like a river.
   (Psalm 105:41)

God of wonderful works,
   glory be to your name.

When your children were slaves,
   you set them free.
When your children were thirsty,
   you cracked open the rock in the desert.
When your children were hungry,
   you sent quails from the sky
   and bread from the heavens.
And when your children came to the land of milk
   and honey,
   you made it home.

God of the promised land,
   glory be to your name.
Come, make a home with your children.

Awesome

The LORD is gracious and merciful. (Psalm 111:4b)

Holy and awesome God,

We thank you at table today
    for grace,
and we thank you at table today
    for mercy.

We praise you at table today
    for your justice,
and we praise you at table today
    for your faithfulness.

We thank you at table today
    for good food to eat;
and we praise you at table today
    for good company to strengthen our hearts.

Holy and awesome God,
    we thank and praise you forever.

Help

I lift up my eyes to the hills—
from where will my help come? (Psalm 121:1)

Holy Creator, maker of heaven and hill, earth and valley,
    keep our lives away from evil, we pray,
    as we face the heat of the day
and as we sleep in the shadows of the moon;
    keep our hearts grateful,
as we share our meals and as we rest easy;
    keep our feet steady,
as we come into our home and as we go out again;
    keep our lips praising you,
as we work and as we play;
    keep our lives away from evil, we pray,
now and forever.

A Weaned Child

But I have calmed and quieted my soul,
  like a weaned child with its mother.
  (Psalm 131:2a)

Holy God,
      who nurtures our lives with hope,
            calm our thoughts for now,
            and quiet our souls.

Let us enjoy the good food before us.
Let us enjoy the good company of this home.
Let us enjoy a good time and not hurry.

Calm our thoughts and quiet our souls,
      Holy God, so we can rest in you.

Family

How very good and pleasant it is
  when kindred live together in unity!
  (Psalm 133:1)

O God of the blessing,
    bring us together, we pray;
    unite our family by your goodness,
    and knit us tightly by your mercy.

Anoint this table with love, Holy One,
    and pour your blessing like soft oil
    over the face of the earth.

Drench all the families of earth in blessing.
Bring us together, we pray, and let us live.

An Open Hand

The eyes of all look to you,
    and you give them their food in due season.
(Psalm 145:15)

God of grace and God of mercy,
we praise you this day and every day,
    blessing your name
    from one generation to the next,
    forever and ever.

Open your hand, compassionate One,
    and feed the world with the fruits of the
    season.
Open your hand, awesome One,
    and bless us all with your steadfast love.

God of grace and God of mercy,
    we praise you this day and every day.

Section II

Devotional Prayers of Joy and Care

Introduction to Devotional Prayers

After breathing in the good things flowing from God—the fruits of the earth, the love known around a table, the grace nourishing life together—we breathe out. Care and compassion, as well as hope and joy, are some of the ways the psalms direct our breathing, and therefore, our lives. Devotional prayers are the lifeblood of devotional acts.

The psalms are often extremely attentive to places where love is lacking and suffering is not. It could be the psalmist who is in pain or being persecuted; it could just as easily be those whom the psalmists see and the world does not: orphans on the street, widows left with nothing, prisoners, the sick, victims of war, and more. The psalms make abundantly clear that the strength to face such difficulties is itself a gift from God's hand, whether the trouble is in our own lives or in matters of the larger world. The strength flows from the deepest kind of hope, a secure sense that, as Psalm 30:5 puts it, *Weeping may linger for the night, but joy comes with the morning.*

So the psalms move about easily between praise and concern, glory and trouble, heaven and earth. The logic is radically simple: fed, we feed others; blessed, we bless others; cared for, we care for others; loved, we love others.

Like the psalmists, we too have troubles and celebrations to share with the Holy One. While the following prayers can stand alone, they also make room for any particular joys and concerns you may have. Whether concluding a meal or at some other moment in the day, devotional times are good opportunities to open our hearts, unscripted, with the One whose heart is devoted to the world.

In the end, the ability to praise and the ability to care are rooted in the same soil. The soil is somewhere deep in our souls, a place God nears. Sensing proximity to the Holy, the soul cannot contain itself any more than the lungs of a newborn can contain the first breath of life.

Beating Hearts

I will give thanks to the LORD with my whole heart;
I will tell of all your wonderful deeds. (Psalm 9:1)

O God of wonder,
    as you bring joy from sorrow,
    and life from the pit of suffering,
    every heart beats praise to you—
    each heartbeat is a thanksgiving.

You hold us when days are hard.
You make us grateful when days are easy.
You find the lost.
You shelter the poor.
You love abandoned children.
You remember the forgotten.

Every heart beats praise to you, mighty God,
    each heartbeat is a thanksgiving.

[Naming particular joys or concerns aloud or in
silent meditation would be very appropriate before
ending these devotional prayers.]

Rise Up

Rise up, O LORD; O God, lift up your hand;
do not forget the oppressed. (Psalm 10:12)

God of justice,
    hear our prayer and rise up, we pray.
Remember brokenhearted people
    and provide them strength.
Listen to the orphans of the world
    and answer their cries.
See the helpless
    and lend your support.
God of the troubled,
    hear our prayer and rise up.
Remember oppressed people
    and provide release.
Listen to those filled with grief
    and offer comfort.
See the evil threatening life
    and break it.
God of justice,
    let our prayers and your hand
    make us bold enough to rise up
    and follow you.

Ancestors

In you our ancestors trusted;
*   they trusted, and you delivered them.*
*   (Psalm 22:4)*

God of the generations,
    for thousands of years
    our ancestors have cried out to you and
        been saved.
For generations and generations
    your people have trusted you for life.
You feed the hungry until satisfied.
You show your face to those in pain.
You turn the cries of terror
    into whoops of praise.
God of glory,
    we join our voices with those of the past to
        praise you;
    we join our praises with the generations
        to come,
        worshiping you.
Neither life nor death can stop us.

Open the Gates

The earth is the Lord's and all that is in it,
the world, and those who live in it. (Psalm 24:1)

Where do you dwell, O God of glory,
and where is your blessing?

Our massive doors and strongest gates
cannot contain your majesty.
False hearts and deceptive words
only hide us from your face—
they are nothing.

O God of all creation,
open the gates!
Fling the doors wide,
and let oceans and rivers
sparkle with your glory.

Bless the world, we pray.
Free up every heart!
Lift our souls, and let the earth
shine with blessing.

Steadfast Love

*Be mindful of your mercy, O LORD, and of your
steadfast love,
for they have been from of old. (Psalm 25:6)*

O God of Israel,
    we give you thanks for your steadfast love,
      for the grace that is so old, so sure, and so good
        that we bow humbled.

The lonely, you befriend.
The burdened heart, you relieve.
The distressed, you deliver.
The forgotten, you remember.
The lost, you guide.
The sinner, you forgive.
The vulnerable, you guard.
The captured, you free.

O God our redeemer,
    we give you thanks for your steadfast love,
      for the grace that is so old, so sure, and so good
        that we bow humbled.

Joy in the Morning

Weeping may linger for the night,
  but joy comes with the morning. (Psalm 30:5b)

O LORD our God,
    we will give thanks to you forever.
You heal our wounded hearts
    and give us life.
You hear our cries
    and raise us from the pit of death,
        from dust,
            from the grave of despair.
O LORD our God,
    we will give thanks to you forever.
You take away our grief
    and give us joy.
You turn mourning into dancing,
    ashes into stars,
    silence into praise.
O LORD our God,
    we will give thanks to you forever.
We will give thanks to you forever.

A New Song

A king is not saved by his great army;
a warrior is not delivered by his great strength.
(Psalm 33:16)

With a word from God, the heavens are born.
With a breath, the angels and stars and more.
God sings out the earth and all creation
    with the melody of love and the rhythms of grace.
So break out the drums and the harps.
Make trumpets and cymbals shout.
Let melody and rhythm join all the voices of God's people
    to sing a new song.
Great nations are nothing.
Powerful leaders are fools.
Mighty weapons are vanities.
Strong warriors can never save us.
They all return to death.
Only the song of love, only the rhythms of grace,
    can help us, can save us,
      can free us, can liven up our hearts.
Let the world dance!

Righteousness

Then I will thank you in the great congregation;
   in the mighty throng I will praise you.
   (Psalm 35:18)

O God of righteousness,
   who on this earth is like you?

While the world worships strength,
   you deliver the weak.
While humanity loves wealth,
   you treasure those in need.
While evil thrives on power and slippery words,
   you, great God, rescue the vulnerable,
   restore broken lives,
   and remember righteousness.

Let the world worship the LORD.
Let humanity love the Holy One.
Let evil dry up and blow away
   like chaff in the wind.

Our tongues will tell your righteousness, Holy God,
   praising you and praising you more.

City of God

"Be still, and know that I am God!"
   (Psalm 46:10a)

O God, our present help,
   lead us to the river of celebration,
   the waters streaming through
      the city of God.
Times are troubled—
   nations roar like the lion;
   kingdoms crack and crash;
   and the earth itself cries for help.
O God our refuge,
   make it stop!
Break the bow and rifle.
Shatter the spear and missile.
Burn the shield and tank.
Make it all stop to the ends of the earth.
O God of life,
   lead us to the riverside
   where peace flows,
   and the world knows
that you are God.

Rebuilding

Restore to me the joy of your salvation,
and sustain in me a willing spirit. (Psalm 51:12)

Have mercy, O God,
    have mercy upon us today.
Without you our hearts are empty
    and our bones ache.
Without your presence we fall apart.
Rebuild us, Holy God,
rebuild all the broken places
    in this world,
    in our homes,
    in our hearts.
May your steadfast love
    wash over the earth.
May your Holy Spirit
    refresh every broken spirit.
May your wisdom
    teach us the power of joy.
Rebuild us with mercy, we pray.
Open our lips and free our tongues
    to praise you.

Olive Tree

But I am like a green olive tree
  in the house of God.
I trust in the steadfast love of God
  forever and ever. (Psalm 52:8)

Good and mighty God,
    for the steadfast love that holds us,
    we will thank you forever.

Help us to trust you and your love alone—
    not wealth or riches,
    not plots or plans,
    not words or ideas
    blinding us from the truth of your love.

Plant us, instead,
    like an olive tree in your house,
    growing in love forever.

Good and mighty God,
    we praise your name.

Let It Rain Down

You visit the earth and water it,
  you greatly enrich it;
the river of God is full of water;
  you provide the people with grain. (Psalm 65:9)

O God of our salvation,

> You are the hope of the earth,
> the strength of the mountains,
> the joy of morning and night.

Valleys and meadows sing for you;
  hills and fields shout;
  streams and rivers overflow with praise.

Let it rain down.
Let blessing flow everywhere.

Bless Every Nation

Let the nations be glad and sing for joy,
for you judge the peoples with equity
and guide the nations upon earth. (Psalm 67:4)

God of the earth,
 face the people around this globe,
 and shine like the sun.
Bless every nation in the world,
 and let them sing.

You are the God of grace.
You are the God of blessing.
You are the God of a world made good.

Warm the earth with your face, we pray.
Shine joy upon people everywhere.

Scattered

Summon your might, O God;
show your strength, O God, as you have done for
us before. (Psalm 68:28)

God of power and majesty,
you are awesome in your sanctuary
and majestic on your mountain.

Before you, the earth quakes,
and the heavens pour rain;
evil scatters, running for cover,
as kings and armies flee.

Blessed is God, the fountain of life,
who protects widows and is a father to
orphans,
who leads prisoners to prosperity
and scatters to the wind all who love war.

Let the heavens dance and the earth sing.
Let the universe parade in thanksgiving.

Drowning

Save me, O God,
for the waters have come up to my neck.
(Psalm 69:1)

O Holy One of Israel,
 accept the praise from our lips
 and the thanksgiving in our hearts
 as an offering to you.
You deliver the brokenhearted people of this world.
You hear the needy in our streets.
You bring joy to oppressed people everywhere.
Accept the praise from our lips
 and the thanksgiving in our hearts
 as an offering to you.
You rescue all who are sinking in the mire of hatred,
 and show your face for love's sake.
You hear our cries of drowning and come quickly.
Accept the praise from our lips
 and the thanksgiving in our hearts
 as an offering to you.

God Is Great

Let all who seek you
*   rejoice and be glad in you.*
Let those who love your salvation
*   say evermore, "God is great!" (Psalm 70:4)*

O God of our salvation,
    for delivering your people,
        you are great!
    for hastening to help the persecuted,
        you are great!
    for confusing those who threaten and hurt us,
        you are great!
    for saving the poor,
        you are great!
    for rushing to the needy,
        O God, you are great!

We join all who love your salvation
    to say evermore, "God is great!"

Peace

May there be abundance of grain in the land;
may it wave on the tops of the mountains;
may its fruit be like Lebanon;
and may people blossom in the cities
like the grass of the field. (Psalm 72:16)

O God of abundant life,
may your glory fill every land
and your justice rule the nations;
may prosperity rain down from the heavens
and peace blossom in every field upon
the earth.

Deliver those who cry, we pray.
Break oppression and violence with love.
Feed every poor child under the sun—
help all in need—
and let peace flow from sea to sea.

Blessed be the God of abundance,
whose peace will never end.

Creation

*Do not deliver the soul of your dove to the
wild animals;
do not forget the life of your poor forever.
(Psalm 74:19)*

O God of creation,
remember your people—the slaves of Egypt—
    you delivered long ago;
remember your mountain—the place heaven
    and earth meet—where you came to dwell;
remember your sanctuary—the holy place—
    burned and destroyed by enemies of creation.
How long, O God,
    will the dove be at risk?
How long will violence fill the earth?
Yet you endure from old, Holy One.
Your love creates a new day,
    a day filled with ever-flowing streams
    and creatures of every kind.
You dry up hatred, and flood destruction with goodness.
Rise up, O God, and create.
Renew this day,
    and let every dove fly to your glory.

Exodus

Your way was through the sea,
your path, through the mighty waters;
yet your footprints were unseen. (Psalm 77:19)

Mighty God of the exodus,
the wonders of your hand
 comfort our souls
    and breathe life into our spirits.
Before you, seas tremble, and the earth shakes.

Hear the cries of those who are troubled, we pray.
Calm the thoughts of those who are afraid.
Lead all those who grieve into new life.

Mighty God of the exodus,
as the waters of cruelty part and the path of
        compassion becomes solid,
    we remember your love;
    we rejoice in your grace; and
    we recognize the power
that makes the world tremble.

Seeing

Restore us, O God;
let your face shine, that we may be saved.
(Psalm 80:3)

O Shepherd of Israel,
shine your face upon us,
and lead us again to good ground.

Shine your face upon all who pray for help
and those who have lost hope.
Shine your face upon all who feed on the bread
of tears,
those who are broken and scorned
and full of pain.

Turn your face to the earth, O God of hosts,
and see the lost and the homeless.
See all who are hidden
from the eyes of the world.

Shine your face, Holy One,
and help us see.

Learning to Walk

Teach me your way, O LORD,
that I may walk in your truth;
give me an undivided heart to revere your name.
(Psalm 86:11)

O God of steadfast love,
  trusting you, we devote our hearts
  to learning and our lives to walking.

Teach us truth, that we may walk with courage.
Teach us mercy, that we may walk with humility.
Teach us forgiveness, that we may walk with compassion.
Teach us grace, that we may walk with strength.
Teach us wonder, that we may walk with praise.
Teach us goodness, that we may walk with those in need.

O God of steadfast love,
  learning from you, may we walk well.

The Home of All People

Glorious things are spoken of you,
O city of God. (Psalm 87:3)

Holy God, Most High, who gives birth to every nation,
establish the city of your glory, we pray.

Open the gates to home, the home of all people,
the place where enemies gather to sing praises,
the place where hostile nations learn to dance
together.

Establish the city, we pray,
the springs of life
where all the families of the earth are blessed
and claim the city of God as home.

Troubles

For my soul is full of troubles,
and my life draws near to Sheol. (Psalm 88:3)

O God of salvation,
   lean in, we pray, and listen to the cries.

Hear the prayer of troubled souls:
   those facing death,
   the helpless,
   the forgotten,
   those overwhelmed by grief,
   the rejected,
   the imprisoned,
   the desperate.

O God of salvation,
   lean in and listen.
Hear the cries from the Pit.

Compassion

Before the mountains were brought forth,
*   or ever you had formed the earth and the world,*
*   from everlasting to everlasting you are God.*
*   (Psalm 90:2)*

O God of Moses,
    let your favor rest upon us,
    and bless the world for a thousand years—
    and a million more.

How long will evil thrive
    and hatred flourish?
How long does it take for compassion
    to rule humanity's heart and the souls of nations?

Sweep sin away like a bad dream, we pray,
    and let joy prosper
    and never fade away.
May the morning of your steadfast love
    come quickly.
May the day soon break,
    filled with the glad faces
    of thriving babies and flourishing children.

Shelter

You will not fear the terror of the night,
*   or the arrow that flies by day. (Psalm 91:5)*

In the shelter of your presence we pray,
    almighty God, in the refuge
    of your dwelling place.
Bring courage to those
    who tremble by day and fear the night.
Cover them with your protective wings,
    and let your angels guard every troubled child.
Rescue this world
    from terror,
    from pestilence,
    from every arrow of hatred.
Deliver this world with love,
    and satisfy us with life.
Be at home with us,
Most High, be our shelter,
    we pray.

Rock for Joy

*Then shall all the trees of the forest sing for joy.
  (Psalm 96:12b)*

Come righteous judge,
    and let your glory shine forever.

The heavens are sparkling with delight,
    while the earth rocks for joy.
Critters and creatures of every kind cry,
    "Hallelujah!"
    while green grasslands flow with praise.

The trees are singing.
The seas are shouting.
Birds and bugs jump,
    while fish fly through the air.

Come, Holy God.
Come, let us praise you.

God Is Near

Let the floods clap their hands;
let the hills sing together for joy. (Psalm 98:8)

Rivers rush their banks and flood the ground with
    power—
    justice is near.
Mountains are moving and glaciers stepping
    back—
    fairness is on the way.
The earth is shaking and the moon glowing with
    glory—
    love is approaching.

The universe and everything in it
    prepares to worship God.

Joy to creation, we are set right.

Praise the Holy One.

Faithful

Make a joyful noise to the LORD, all the earth.
  (Psalm 100:1)

In every age, our shepherd is faithful.
To all generations, our maker is good.

From the first day to the last,
    the love of God never dies.
From the light of creation,
    to the day of good rest,
    the love of God lives forever.

May every age be grateful.
May all generations make a joyful noise.

To Live Secure

The children of your servants shall live secure;
their offspring shall be established in your presence.
(Psalm 102:28)

Holy God of Jerusalem, maker of heaven and earth,
    may children a thousand years from now
    proclaim the truth:
how you hear the groans of the imprisoned;
how you attend to the prayers of the destitute;
how you release the doomed
and lift up those crushed to dust.

O God of compassion,
    renew heaven and earth by your creative hand.
Reshape this generation
    to hear the imprisoned,
    to attend to the destitute,
    to release the doomed,
    to lift up the crushed.

May your children live secure.

Steady

They are not afraid of evil tidings;
their hearts are firm, secure in the LORD.
(Psalm 112:7)

Secure our hearts, Holy One,
and bless this generation.

Steady us, we pray, and keep us faithful:
to give freely to the poor,
to delight in your commandments,
to do business for the sake of justice,
to live by grace and generosity.

Steady us, we pray, to fear no evil.
Secure our hearts, Holy One,
and bless this world.

Harvest

May those who sow in tears
reap with shouts of joy. (Psalm 126:5)

O God of the harvest,
    restore the fortunes of lands dried out by sadness.
Gather the tears of your people everywhere,
    and water the desert for a new season.

Restore laughter to those who grieve.
Bring good dreams to those who need relief.
Send hope to hearts broken and lost.

Let there be a new harvest, mighty God.
Let there be a new harvest of joy
    to fill every mouth with praise.

Redemption

Out of the depths I cry to you, O LORD.
(Psalm 130:1)

Hear the cry of our souls, O Redeemer;
in your mercy, hear the cries of the world.

Untwist our tangled ways, we pray.
Untie the knots of hatred choking the nations.

Release in our world a longing for redemption,
and free our souls to seek the way of love,
every morning, every night, every moment.

In you we set our hopes and our fears, mighty God.
For you the world waits.

Bowing

I bow down toward your holy temple
and give thanks to your name for your steadfast
love and your faithfulness. (Psalm 138:2a)

We give you thanks, glorious one,
    for your mercy endures forever.

May all the rulers on earth bow
    to your steadfast love.
May the whole world praise
    the work of your hands.

You lift the lowly and humble the haughty.
You strengthen the weak and exhaust the mighty.
You deliver the troubled and plague the powerful.

We bow in praise to you, loving God,
    and pray your ways
    are fulfilled in all places.
May your steadfast love
    endure forever.

Wonderful

I praise you, for I am fearfully and wonderfully made.
Wonderful are your works;
that I know very well. (Psalm 139:14)

O God of the light,
the works of your hands
    are wonderful,
    amazing to see,
    and overwhelming to imagine.
The light of each day
    startles our eyes
    and awakens our souls to your presence.
The darkness of each night
    softens our minds
    and frees our bodies to rest in your presence.
From the outer edges of the universe
    to the inner reaches of our thoughts,
    you are there, breathing life.
Before the beginning, beyond the end,
    you are there.
Wonderful are your works.

Mercy

*I know that the LORD maintains the cause of the needy,
and executes justice for the poor. (Psalm 140:12)*

Hear, Holy God, a cry for mercy.
Deliver your creatures from the hand of evil,
    and protect people everywhere from violence.
Guard the world, we pray, from the poison
    of lies, arrogance, and slander
    that infects children with hatred
    and nations with war.

Hear, Holy God, a cry.
Let evil fall into its own trap.
Bury wicked ways deep into the earth
    to be forgotten forever.
Raise up the poor,
    carry the needy on your back,
    and let righteousness loose everywhere.

Holy God, hear our cry for mercy.

Maker

Do not put your trust in princes,
in mortals, in whom there is no help.
(Psalm 146:3)

Hallelujah!
Praise the holy name of God,
maker of heaven and earth.

As the plots of the powerful perish,
as the schemes of rulers turn to dust,
there stands the One who reigns forever,
keeping faith with us:
freeing prisoners,
watching over foreigners,
executing justice for those wronged,
giving vision to the blind,
lifting those who are lonely and abandoned.

Praise the holy name of God,
maker of heaven and earth.
Hallelujah!

Praise

Praise the LORD, O Jerusalem!
Praise your God, O Zion! (Psalm 147:12)

Hallelujah!
Praise the holy name of God,
    who brings refugees home and food to
        the hungry,
    who heals broken hearts and tends
        the wounded,
    who blows the spirit to every troubled place.

Hallelujah!
Praise the holy name of God,
    who numbers the stars and stirs the oceans,
    who cares for each bird and feeds wild
        animals,
    who bathes the earth with justice and grace.

Hallelujah!
Praise the holy name of God.

Hallelujah!

Let everything that breathes praise the LORD!
Praise the LORD! (Psalm 150:6)

Hallelujah!
Praise the holy name of God.

With the deepest breath
    and the power of joy,
    we cry, "Hallelujah!"

Songs and dances are praising God.
Drums and pipes are praising God.
Strings and brass and keys and voices
    are praising God.
Care and kindness, love and justice,
    compassion and hope,
 deeds and respect are praising God like wild.

"Let everything that breathes praise the LORD!"
Hallelujah!

Memory Bedtime Prayers

Night-Light

(Inspired by Psalm 4)

O God of light,
    your face is so bright
      that we smile through the night.

Let it shine.
Let it shine.
Let it shine.

Sweeter than Honey

(Inspired by Psalm 19)

Sweeter than honey,
    brighter than the sun,
      bigger than the sky at night,
O God, you're the One.

Bless the World

(Inspired by Psalm 24)

Bless the world,
    and let it glow
with holy love
    for all to know. *[God bless…]*

Good Sleep

(Inspired by Psalm 30)

For good sleep at night
    and joy with the day,
    my soul thanks you God,
    at rest and at play.

Clap for Joy

(Inspired by Psalm 47)

God is awesome
    clap for joy. *[clap once]*
God is awesome,
    clap again. *[clap twice]*
Amen. *[clap three times]*

Thank God

(Inspired by Psalm 52)

We thank God for love.
We thank God for life.
We thank God for everything.
We thank God tonight.
    [Thank you, God, for…]

Nest

(Inspired by Psalm 84)

As the bird finds a home
    where her children can nest,
my heart finds in you God
    a good place to rest.

Sleep Tight

(Inspired by Psalm 97)

With the sight of the night,
    with sleep ever so tight,
    with the dawn of new light,
    we praise God with delight.

Hallelujah, Amen!

(Inspired by Psalm 148)

The stars do a dance
　　while the moon sings a hymn
　　to praise our Creator.
Hallelujah, amen!

Index of Psalms

Index of Psalms